This is a work of fiction. Names, characters, places and incidents are the product of the author's imagination or are used fictitiously. Any resemblance to actual persons, living or dead, events, or locations is entirely coincidence.

Text copyright 2016 by Teresha Rue-Hughes
Cover art, interior illustrations copyright 2016 by Teresha Rue-Hughes

All rights reserved.
Published in the United States by Sungi Bear LLC

Visit us at www.Sungibear.com
For further information
Email: sungibear@gmail.com

The Sungi Bear Collection
Sungi Bear and Friends Journal of Dreams: Sungi Bear and his friends want to help you take the right steps towards your dreams.

ISBN # 9780692712252

Printed in the United States of America

The Sungi Bear Collection

1. *Where is Sungi Bear?*
2. *Sungi Bear Makes New Friends*
3. *Sungi Bear and Friends Journal of Dreams-Journal*

Table of Contents

1. Introduction: Letter to Young Journalist 1

2. Letter to Parents/Guardians and Teachers 2

3. Sight Words 3

4. Sungi Bear: Tell me about you 4-9

5. Saadiah: What do you like to do for fun? 10-15

6. Elijah: What is the best career for you? 16-21

7. The Twins: How can you make the world better? 22-27

8. Ricky: What do you fear? 28-33

9. Lorenzo: What would you do if you were bullied? 34-39

10. This Is My Final Career Choice 40

11. Baby Steps 41

12. A Small List of Possible Career Choices 42

Lorenzo   Samya   Lailah   Sungi Bear   Ricky   Saadiah   Elijah

Introduction

Dear Young Journalist,

We, Sungi Bear and friends, are here to help you take the right steps towards a bright future.

With this journal, we will ask you some questions and you can answer the questions with words and pictures. This journal will help you, your parents/guardians and your teachers see what you do well and where you need more help.

Soon, with this journal, and the help of me, Sungi Bear, my friends, and your parents/guardians and teachers, you will be off to making your best future and reaching your hopes and dreams. Cheers to a bright future!

"What Can You Imagine?!"

Sincerely,
Sungi Bear and Friends

Lorenzo   Samya   Lailah   Sungi Bear   Ricky   Saadiah   Elijah

Dear Parents and Guardians,

The purpose of this journal is to help you understand and expand upon your child's likes, dislikes, strengths, weaknesses, desires and goals. This Journal will get your child started on the path to making decisions and planning for their future, early!

Dear Teachers,

This journal will help increase your understanding of each child as an individual. This journal will also aid in your building on their strengths and understanding their weaknesses.

The way to use this journal is simple:

- *Explain the purpose of this journal to your child/student*
- *Discuss the weekly question with them*
- *Have them answer the question and draw a matching picture*
- *Discuss their answer and picture*
- *Date and sign each page*
- *Complete one page each week in each section and then do each section again until the book is complete*
- *Do page 40 last*
- *Refer back to the journal as needed*
- *Get extra journals for continued growth*

This journal will help increase your child/student's confidence and self-esteem as well as expose them to expressive writing and critical thinking. Working in this journal weekly and having a discussion will bring out some great talking points. Sungi Bear and his friends are here to help you every step of the way!

Lorenzo   Samya   Lailah   Sungi Bear   Ricky   Saadiah   Elijah

Sight Words

Grade: K	Grade: 1	Grade: 2
a	after	always
and	any	because
away	ask	before
can	by	best
come	could	does
find	every	first
for	from	found
funny	going	gave
go	had	many
good	just	read
help	know	right
here	let	sleep
jump	once	those
like	over	use
new	some	very
please	take	which
ride	then	wish
saw	think	would
soon	walk	write
went	when	your

Lorenzo   Samya   Lailah   Sungi Bear   Ricky   Saadiah   Elijah

Hi, I am Sungi Bear. I live with my mom and dad and I have a cat named Friskus. I also have a great imagination. It helps me think of many good things to do.

Tell me about you.

Sungi Bear

On the next few pages, tell me about you. Draw some pictures.

Tell me about you.

Date: _____
Teacher: _____
Parent/Guardian: _____

Tell me about you?

Date: _____
Teacher: _____
Parent/Guardian: _____

Tell me about you?

_____

- -

_____

- -

_____

- -

_____

Date: _____

Teacher: _____

Parent/Guardian: _____

Tell me about you?

_____
- -
_____

_____
- -
_____

_____
- -
_____

Date: _____

Teacher: _____

Parent/Guardian: _____

Tell me about you?

_____

_____

_____

_____

Date: _____

Teacher: _____

Parent/Guardian: _____

Hi, I am Saadiah.
I like to design clothes and play dress-up for fun.

Tell me what you like to do for fun.

Saadiah

On the next few pages, tell me about some things you like to do for fun. Draw some pictures.

What do you like to do for fun?

Date: _____

Teacher: _____

Parent/Guardian: _____

What do you like to do for fun?

_____
_____
_____
_____
_____
_____

Date: _____

Teacher: _____

Parent/Guardian: _____

What do you like to do for fun?

Date: _____
Teacher: _____
Parent/Guardian: _____

What do you like to do for fun?

Date: _____

Teacher: _____

Parent/Guardian: _____

What do you like to do for fun?

_____
- - - - - - - - - - - - - - - -
_____

_____
- - - - - - - - - - - - - - - -
_____

_____
- - - - - - - - - - - - - - - -
_____

Date: _____
Teacher: _____
Parent/Guardian: _____

Hi, I am Elijah.
When I grow up, I want to be a Policeman.
I like to keep people safe.

What do you want to be when you grow up?

Elijah

On the next few pages, tell me what you want to be when you grow up. Draw some pictures.

What do you want to be when you grow up?

_____

_____

_____

_____

_____

_____

Date: _____

Teacher: _____

Parent/Guardian: _____

What do you want to be when you grow up?

_____

_____

_____

_____

Date: _____
Teacher: _____
Parent/Guardian: _____

What do you want to be when you grow up?

Date: _____

Teacher: _____

Parent/Guardian: _____

What do you want to be when you grow up?

_____
_____
_____
_____

Date: _____
Teacher: _____
Parent/Guardian: _____

What do you want to be when you grow up?

_____
_____
_____
_____
_____
_____

Date: _____
Teacher: _____
Parent/Guardian: _____

Hi, we are The Twins, Samya and Lailah.
I am Samya and I love animals, so I can help teach people how to care for them.
I am Lailah and I pay attention to good eating habits, so I can help the world eat healthier.

Tell us how you can make the world better.

Samya and Lailah

On the next few pages, tell us how you can make the world better. Draw some pictures.

How can you make the world better?

Date: _____
Teacher: _____
Parent/Guardian: _____

How can you make the world better?

_____

_____

_____

_____

_____

_____

Date: _____

Teacher: _____

Parent/Guardian: _____

How can you make the world better?

_____
- - - - - - - - - - - - - - - - - -
_____

_____
- - - - - - - - - - - - - - - - - -
_____

_____
- - - - - - - - - - - - - - - - - -
_____

Date: _____
Teacher: _____
Parent/Guardian: _____

How can you make the world better?

Date: _____
Teacher: _____
Parent/Guardian: _____

How can you make the world better?

_____
- -
_____
- -
_____
- -
_____

Date: _____

Teacher: _____

Parent/Guardian: _____

Hi, I am Ricky.
I fear speaking in front of a lot of people.

Tell me about some things you fear.

Ricky

On the next few pages, tell me about some things you fear. Draw some pictures.

What do you fear?

Date: _____
Teacher: _____
Parent/Guardian: _____

What do you fear?

_____

_____

_____

_____

Date: _____

Teacher: _____

Parent/Guardian: _____

What do you fear?

Date: _____

Teacher: _____

Parent/Guardian: _____

What do you fear?

Date: _____
Teacher: _____
Parent/Guardian: _____

What do you fear?

Date: _____

Teacher: _____

Parent/Guardian: _____

Hi, I am Lorenzo.
I was once bullied and I told my mom.

What would you do if you were ever bullied?

Lorenzo

On the next few pages, tell me what you would do if you were ever bullied. Draw some pictures.

What would you do if you were bullied?

_____
_____
_____
_____
_____
_____
_____

Date: _____
Teacher: _____
Parent/Guardian: _____

What would you do if you were bullied?

_____

_____

_____

_____

_____

_____

Date: _____

Teacher: _____

Parent/Guardian: _____

What would you do if you were bullied?

Date: _____
Teacher: _____
Parent/Guardian: _____

What would you do if you were bullied?

Date: _____

Teacher: _____

Parent/Guardian: _____

What would you do if you were bullied?

_____
- -
_____

_____
- -
_____

_____
- -
_____

Date: _____
Teacher: _____
Parent/Guardian: _____

"What Can You Imagine?!"

What do you imagine being when you grow up?

Did you complete the journal?
Now draw a picture of yourself all grown up in your career.

Date:_____

Teacher:_____

Parent/Guardian:_____

Baby Steps

Reaching your dreams takes determination and will-power.  It also takes you doing research to find out who you are and what makes you, YOU! This means you must keep a journal of all your likes, dislikes, trials and errors.

Remember, it takes small steps to reach big goals. So be patient with yourself and those around you.

A small list of possible career choices:

- Accountant
- Actor
- Anthropologist
- Architect
- Astronaut
- Astronomer
- Biologist
- Brain Surgeon
- Chef
- Chemical Engineer
- Chemist
- Computer Programmer
- Construction Worker
- Dancer
- Dentist
- Director (Business, Movie or TV)
- Doctor
- Electrician
- Engineer
- Entrepreneur
- Fashion designer
- Firefighter
- Florist
- Graphic Designer
- Hairstylist
- Journalist
- Judge
- Lawyer
- Musician (Instrumental or Singer)
- Mayor
- Mechanic
- Pharmacist
- Photographer
- Physical Therapist
- Pilot
- Police Officer
- Politician
- Plumber
- President
- Producer (TV or Movie)
- Psychologist
- Scientist
- Teacher
- Writer
- Veterinarian

Lorenzo   Samya   Lailah   Sunqi Bear   Ricky   Saadiah   Elijah

www.ingramcontent.com/pod-product-compliance
Lightning Source LLC
Chambersburg PA
CBHW051959290426
44110CB00015B/2306